to: Olivia

from: Sheena

Merry Christmas. Enjoy!

Believe
in your
DREAMS

Published by Sellers Publishing, Inc.

161 John Roberts Road, South Portland, ME 04106

Visit us at www.sellerspublishing.com • E-mail: rsp@rsvp.com

© 2016 Sellers Publishing, Inc.

Art and design © 2016 Julissa Mora
Courtesy of Pink Light Studio

Compiled by Robin Haywood

ISBN-13: 978-1-4162-4575-9

Printed and bound in China.

10 9 8 7 6 5 4 3 2 1

Believe in your Dreams

art & design by Julissa Mora

SELLERS
PUBLISHING

is

REAL

— Pablo Picasso

Believe *in your* DREAMS

No MAtter how IMPOSSIBLe they SEEM

– Walt Disney

WHEN
there are
footprints
on the MOON

– Paul Brandt

Not an echo

– Albert Einstein

The biggest Adventure you can take...

Cultivate WONDER...

and LeaRn HOW to BE gentle with YOURSelF

– Anonymous

DO WHAT YOU CAN.

– Arthur Ashe

COURAGE
is not
the absence
of fear,

but

the triUMPH

OVER IT

– Nelson Mandela

and WIN
WHAT YOUR
happy HEART
Desires

– Roel van Sleeuwen

Have
COURAGE.

OPEN
your heart
and

listen to

what your

DREAMS

tell you.

– Paolo Coelho

No MATTER
how scary
the road ahead
MAY SEEM...

NEVER
be afraid
to chase
your DREAMS.

– Melaina Rayne

DREAMS,
to come true,
NEED
a good story.
So go
live ONE.

— Vironika Tugaleva

WHY live
a little,

WHEN you can live a lot?

– Brooke Saward

There is
NO GREATER
Gift
you can
receive...

than to HONOR your calling. IT'S WHY you were BORN.

– Oprah

IT already knows WHAT you WANT to BECOME

– Steve Jobs

and THEN CREATE IT with YOUR HANDS.

– Chris Widener

and TRUST IT

– Aaron Sorkin

IT'S a MAtter of Pulling IT into the physical world.

– Sarah Ban Breathnach

IF you
don't turn
YOUR LifE
into a story,

You ARE capable—

of more than YOU think

— Bradley Whitford

IS
throw away
that Store-bought
MAP and BEGIN
to DRAW
YOUR OWN.

– Michael Dell

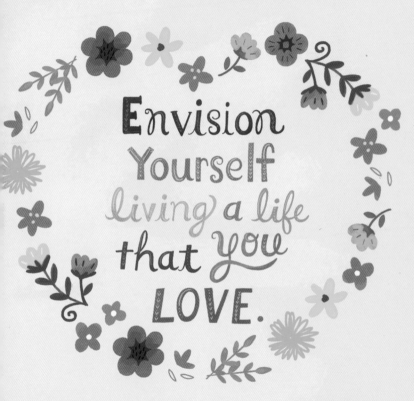

Envision
Yourself
living a life
that you
LOVE.

– Suzan-Lori Parks

It
doesn't MAtter
that your
DREAM came
TRUE

if YOU spent your WHOLE Life sleeping.

– Jerry Zucker

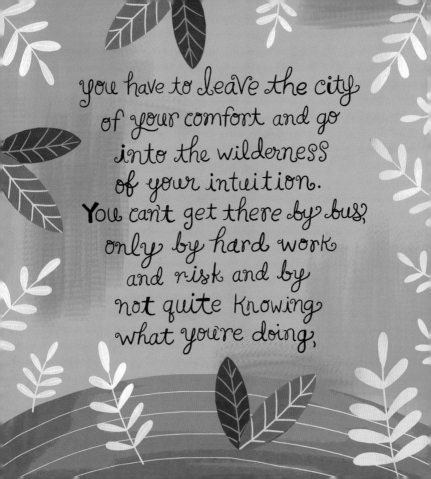

but what
you'll discover
will be
WONDERFUL.
WHAT you'll discover
will Be
YOURSELF.

– Alan Alda

Leave the WORLD more INTERESTING for YOUR BEING HERE.

– Neil Gaiman

Life is Not about warming yourself by the Fire

Life
is about
BUILDING
the Fire

— Larry Luchino

of taking
a misstep
in the
RIGHT
DirecTION.

– Larry Luchino

You have NO Idea
what's GOING to Happen
Next and You Are
mostly just
Making things up
as you GO along.

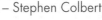
– Stephen Colbert

Life has a very simple plot:

First
you're Here
and then
you're Not.

– Eric Idle

Believe